DON'T BE A

(FILL IN THE BLANK)

WHAT THEY DON'T TELL YOU IN ADMIN SCHOOL:
A GUIDE FOR ASPIRING AND NEW ADMINISTRATORS

KIMIE CARROLL

~ The Staffroom Press ~

Don't Be a __________
What They Don't Tell You in Admin School: A Guide for Aspiring and New Administrators
by Kimie Carroll

Published by The Staffroom Press
Canby, Oregon

ISBN: 979-8-9955783-0-7 (paperback)
ISBN: 979-8-9955783-1-4 (ebook)

Library of Congress Control Number: 2026909279

Printed in the United States of America

First Edition

For my husband John.
He's my everything.

Contents

Acknowledgments

Thank you to my family—John, Mia, Ava, and my beloved parents. Mia and Ava, my sunshine—I could not be prouder of the young women you're becoming.

John, you are my rock. Thank you for dealing with me and my long admin hours for 20 years … wow, you are amazing.

I was ridiculously lucky to spend my career surrounded by incredible people. I tried to sprinkle thank-yous throughout this book, but let's be real—there are hundreds of you who deserve to be named.

YOU are why I stayed in education.

YOU pushed me, challenged me, supported me, and yes, sometimes drove me a little crazy (and vice-versa!)—but all of it made me better.

I learned from the very best. I also learned from the ones who made me think, "What the hell are we doing here?"

Turns out, both are great teachers.

To those I didn't name—don't worry, you're in here. Your fingerprints are all over this book.

I'm grateful for all of it. The good, the bad, and the "are you kidding me?" moments. I wouldn't change a thing.

Preface

Freedom! I just retired after 32 years in education … maybe. I went to administrator school, as I call it, over 25 years ago. Whew! That feels like a lifetime ago. I was a math teacher for almost 12 years and served as a high school associate principal for 20 years. I eventually got tired of working too much and spent 1.5 years as a new teacher mentor.

Along the way, I worked with countless students, families, and staff members, won a few surprising awards, made lots and lots and lots of mistakes, and found successes, learning a ton of lessons each and every year. I wasn't a perfect administrator. Who is? Ha. NO ONE! I learned almost everything about being a great administrator (so I've been told) from the people I served and worked alongside—students, families, staff, and fellow administrators. I did NOT learn quite a bit of that in my master's program in Administrative Studies. I had some amazing professors, but the program didn't reflect what I actually did day to day in real life.

Funny enough, I've heard the same thing from many exceptional administrators. A lot of practical knowledge gets left out of admin programs. Why? Hell if I know! But it made me think it was a good idea to put together a "what I wish I had learned in admin school" book.

I wrote this book because I was NAIVE when I left the dream school where I served as an administrator. I believed all administrators were there for their staff, teachers, parents, students, and communities. I believed they had open minds, kind hearts, and a genuine desire to support teachers so students could succeed. That wasn't the case in my last position as a certified employee (more on that later).

There's a saying in administration, really in management: shit runs downhill. This book is about how not to be that administrator.

While most of my experience is in secondary education, Douglas Reeves told me in an email that my lessons could help elementary school administrators too—so don't worry, this guide has your back no matter the grade level.

Heads up: I cuss. Maybe 20 times. I'm also direct, honest, and occasionally obnoxious. If you're allergic to honesty (or the occasional swear), you might want to skip this one.

If you can handle a little sass with your leadership advice, you're going to be just fine here.

Now, let's goooo!

Kimie

First Page Exercise

Before you start reading this guide, stop for a moment.

When you saw the title *Don't Be a* __________, what word immediately came to mind? Write that word below.

____

Keep that word in the back of your mind as you read.

- That word didn't come out of nowhere.
- It probably came from a boss you had.
- A principal you worked for.
- A district leader you watched struggle.

The truth is, most people go into administration to make things better. Somewhere along the way, good intentions can turn into the very thing teachers fear most.

This guide is a collection of practical lessons from over three decades in education—things that helped build strong schools, and mistakes that taught me what not to do.

Nobody plans to become *that* administrator…

And this book will help you become a leader people actually want to follow.

1

Foundation | Relationships Are KEY

I'm telling you, relationships are KEY. Hard stop. Period. Exclamation point! As the kids would text nowadays, FR (for real). I'm not kidding one bit.

If you're a new or aspiring administrator and you don't believe this, or you aren't open to it, your time in administration will be one long, bumpy, uncomfortable, not-fun, ineffective ride. So where do you start? By getting to know your staff, students, and families. It sounds easy, but it takes a LOT of time. Also, please hear this: you are *not* better than anyone else. I don't know how else to say it. Don't act like a know-it-all, even when the person you're talking to is making zero sense.

I'm especially talking about families. Sometimes they're smelly. Sometimes they don't seem like they care. Sometimes it feels like you have the same conversation over and over, with very little change. If you can remember that they're doing the best they can, that they know their student better than anyone else, and that they do want their student to succeed, you can treat them with respect every single time. Many families carry immense trauma from schools and automatically assume teachers and administrators are a bunch of condescending assholes. They didn't usually say that out loud, but I could tell. I didn't hold it against them.

Side note on the term "families." I'm talking about parents, grandparents, legal guardians. Students don't just have parents. Sometimes they live with an aunt or uncle or even a friend's mom or dad.

So please NOTE: if I write parent, I mean parent/guardian/grandparent/aunt/whomever is in charge of the student.

When I talk about students, I'm talking about middle school and high school students. They aren't stupid. Sometimes adults treat them like they are. John Ogden, former colleague and friend, used to to make fun of me and call me a "long talker" when I met with students and families. Yes, I was a long talker, BUT it saved me time later. I took the time to learn about families and students so I could connect with them. Everyone wants to connect. I treated students like they mattered. Yes, they sometimes aggravated me, but I still liked them as people. I told them that. I also told them when I didn't like their behavior. They understood the difference and we had mutual respect.

And again, remember this: you aren't better than your staff, either. Not everyone has the same education, and not everyone processes information the same way. That's a strength. Different perspectives, different opinions, and a variety of staff members make a school stronger. Not everyone thinks the same, and that's okay. Treat everyone with respect. Get to know your staff so they feel heard and valued. Sometimes the answer is no, and that's normal. I had to say no a lot, and I rarely had issues with staff because of it.

So HOW do you do this? You start by being out and about with kids and staff. Email can wait. Whenever possible, schedule meetings outside of instructional time, unless you're meeting with parents or students.

Your presence matters more than your inbox ever will.

And there's a reason for that—Cal Newport, in *A World Without Email: Reimagining Work in an Age of Communication Overload,* talks about how constant emails and interruptions destroy focus and make work feel chaotic. Being visible, accessible, and human will always matter more than being "caught up" on messages.

Before and After School

Be outside greeting students and parents in different areas of the school. Greet the school bus drivers. Learn their names. Get out in the halls and visit every area of the building. I didn't always get everywhere, and I'd do that differently if I were a new administrator now. John Ogden and I used to meet yearly with our bus drivers to give them a pep talk and share tips on student discipline. It also gave them a chance to know our faces. All four administrators were always out on bus duty after school, and we rotated areas while greeting students before school.

During Passing Time, Lunch, and Recess

Do NOT schedule meetings during these times. We used to compare the bell to Pavlov's dog. Remember classical conditioning from school? When the bell rang, administrators went straight into the halls, each of us to different areas. That presence lets us talk with students and staff, minimize meetings and pull students from class. It helps us get to know more kids, and increase safety just by being there. During lunch, admin would head to the cafeteria for a quick stand-up meeting, usually two or three minutes, then supervise different areas alongside our campus security specialist. It was a great mid-day check-in.

I also visited teachers in their classrooms before school. Teachers had management time, unstructured time we could technically dictate, but we rarely scheduled more than one staff meeting a month. They had about 25 minutes before school that they could use for prep. I would stop in, if they were available, talk with them, and get to know them. I also made it a point to talk with nutrition services staff, secretaries, instructional assistants, and custodial staff.

During Class

Make it a habit to pop in and visit classrooms. Of course, follow any union rules that apply. In my district, we were allowed to visit teachers whenever we wanted. A fun part of my job was coaching teachers and observing them teach. I never wanted teachers to feel afraid when I entered their classroom. It was great to see teachers in "moments in time," working with students, and to help out if needed. Once teachers got to know me better, they started using me as a resource and asked me to come in and gather data for them. It was amazing. We'll talk more about observation and evaluation later.

Be Intentional

Getting to know people has to be real. You have to actually want to know them and understand what makes them tick. The more you know about a person, the easier it is to connect with them. And it works both ways. The more a parent, student, or staff member knows you, the more they can relate to you, like you, and give you grace when things go wrong.

I've heard fellow administrators say they don't want staff members to know too much about them. I'm not saying you should share everything. DUH. But it's important to share yourself, especially with staff. I limited what I shared with students and families, for sure. I never told students exactly what I did when I was very naughty in the '80s. Nope. I told them I wasn't a bad person; I just sometimes made bad choices.

With colleagues, I did share more of myself. For example, I had a really rough month during my last year as an administrator. I took a month off, focused on my mental health, got on some meds, and figured some things out. When I came back, I shared this with my staff when they asked. If I had broken my leg, I would have shared that too. I wasn't ashamed of why I was gone. There's already far too much stigma around mental health. We knew each other as people, not just colleagues. They accepted me and appreciated that transparency.

It's always important to assume the best intentions in people. Yes, that can be hard. It's even harder with people you dislike. I won't pretend I was perfect. Not even close. I did get better the longer I was an administrator, though. In general, people try their best and want to do the right thing. I believe that. Building relationships takes time. It takes years. Don't rush it, and trust that it will be worth it in the end.

For more on leading with clarity, trust, and a little grit, check out *Lead It Like Lasso* by Marnie Stockman, Ed.D., and Nick Coniglio—your no-nonsense guide to getting results, supporting your team, and keeping your sense of humor intact.

What about people you don't like? That can be a challenge. BUT you need to buck up, be a grown-up, be a leader, and fake it. They can NEVER know you don't like them. You can always find one or more things you like about a person. Get to know them. Care about them. If I can do it, you can do it. No one is perfect. You have to give every single person your effort, your dedication, and your support. Believe in every single person. That doesn't mean you don't reprimand them when they mess up. Of course you do. But you give them the same coaching, help, and support you would give anyone else. Be unbiased, at the very least recognize your bias.

2

Communication | Regular, Organized, and Timely

Communication seems easy and straightforward, but it often isn't. Organization is KEY. My focus here is communication with staff, students, and families. When I talk about communication, I mean phone calls, emails, meetings with students and families, and all the general stuff like listening, transparency, openness, and organization. Texting with families or students is a big NO…for obvious reasons. It's important to create boundaries and correspond with them via email, work phone or in person.

It drives me CRAZY when I call, text, or email someone and don't hear back. What in the actual f**k? I think it's incredibly rude. I've heard all the excuses.

"Sorry, I was so busy."

"I didn't get your email."

"Oh, you called? I didn't get the message."

On and on. When I was an administrator, I received about 200 emails a day. *Two hundred.* Our expectation was to respond to emails or phone calls within 24–48 hours. If staff did not know the answer, they were expected to send a quick message saying they'd look into it and get back to the person. It's not that hard. That said, if you aren't organized, it can feel impossible.

Phone Messages and Emails

To keep myself organized with phone calls, I made a phone log. I printed ten single-sided pages, stapled them together, and kept the packet right in front of my phone. It was simple.

I made a Google Sheets phone message template with columns:

- Date
- Time
- Name
- Brief message
- Date and time I called back
- Date and time I left a message
- Notes if I reached the person

I printed a new log when I needed one and saved the old ones with the spiral notebooks where I kept all my meeting notes. In case you were wondering, haha.

I had a process of organizing the log so it was easy to navigate and track calls I had not yet returned or ones I was waiting for an answer from after leaving a message. I left a template in the Appendix.

For email, my district used Gmail. I organized my inbox so the newest emails appeared at the top and unread emails showed in bold. At the beginning of each school year, I updated my labels, which I called folders. I numbered them so they appeared in the order I wanted. I would organize them based on how often I communicated with the different people/departments.

My general Gmail list looked like this:

1. Admin

Principal's Name

Assistant's Name

Assistant Principal's Name

Etc.

2. Departments

Math

Science

Etc. (the top ones are ones I supervised)

3. General

This folder includes emails from families and students, along with other non-departmental communication.

Parents

Students

Middle Schools

Elementary Schools

Other Schools

Etc.

4. District Office (DO)

Superintendent

Superintendent Assistant

HR Director

HR Assistant

Teacher Reimbursement

Special Education (SpED)

5. Graduation

With folders and subfolders since I planned graduation

6. Big Projects, for Ex: Academic Planning Guide

This folder is for large, time-limited projects. When it was time to actively work on something, I renumbered it so it floated to the top of my inbox.

7. Master Schedule

With subfolders since I was in charge of the master schedule. I would also renumber when I was actively working on this project.

8. Online

This folder houses vendor emails and online services. My responses stayed in this folder for easy tracking.

9. Miscellaneous

For HR, I often nested additional labels, like the HR Director, HR Assistant, or Teacher Reimbursement. For large projects, I created a specific label and renumbered it when I needed it higher on the list.

One thing I wish I had done was spend more time learning how to use Gmail features like filters, stars, and indicators. There are great YouTube videos on this. Gmail also now reminds you if someone hasn't responded to an email you sent. That feature came out after I no longer worked there. Dang. It's gold.

I tried to clear my inbox weekly (hahaha). With 200 emails a day, that meant I checked before and after school. I tried to be systematic when checking emails so I didn't miss anything. I responded within 24–48 hours, just like phone messages. If I finished an email thread, I filed it in the appropriate label. If I still needed to do something with it, I left it unbolded in my Inbox. If it was bold, I knew I hadn't looked at it yet or needed to revisit it.

If you receive a long email, just call the person. Follow up with a short email summarizing the conversation if needed. You'll save time and avoid confusion.

It's impossible to read emotion accurately in emails. Honestly, email sucks. More than once, I sent a quick response while in a hurry, and staff later asked if I was upset with them. I wasn't. I was just rushed. Unfortunately, rushed emails can sound terse. Sometimes I handled quick email replies while doing walkthroughs during the day. Two birds, one stone.

Email can turn into a black hole, much like scrolling social media. I came in early and stayed late, and I used that time to clean up my inbox. Do your best not to process email during the school day.

I went to a leadership training where they wanted us to have our assistant read and manage our email to save time. I wasn't a fan of this. What one person might think is unimportant could be something I knew I needed to address. Maybe I'm too controlling, side eye, and maybe I could have let that go. I just didn't want to miss anything or miss an opportunity to connect with the people I worked with and for.

How Decisions Are Made and Communicated

This starts with clearly communicating to staff how decisions are made. Collaboration is extremely important in organizations, but not every decision can or should be collaborative. It's tricky, and the process matters. How decisions are made must be communicated clearly.

In general, we used the following decision-making models with staff:

Staff vote (democratic)

Gather feedback, staff votes, and the majority wins.

Admin asks for input first before deciding (consult)

Gather feedback, discuss it with the leadership group, usually department leaders (DLs), and come to a decision collectively. Some may not agree, but present a united front and back the decision.

Admin makes the call (authoritative)

The administration makes the decision. This usually happens when there's a time constraint or when collaboration isn't ideal.

Think old-school decision-making you see in movies or shows like Abbott Elementary.

We agree as a group (consensus)

This is how we often made decisions at my former school. It takes the longest but results in the greatest staff buy-in.

Once a decision is made, it's important to share the outcome. No one likes giving feedback if nothing is going to be done with that feedback.

Communication Missteps

I saw a big feedback issue often in the last organization I worked for. We would be given surveys and more times than not, the department administration didn't share the findings. I'm not sure the superintendent even knew we were asked to complete them. I'm guessing not.

I was sort of part of another department in the same organization and the transparency and feedback loop there was AMAZING. Seeing both perspectives was eye-opening. In the problematic school, staff either lied on surveys or openly admitted they stopped completing them altogether for three reasons:

1. They had raised concerns for years, nothing changed, and no one followed up.
2. The surveys were poorly written and not truly anonymous because of how the questions were structured.

3. They were scared. They believed administrators could identify who wrote the comments and feared retaliation. They said it had happened before.

Oh. My. Gosh. Totally. Fucked. Up.

This is one of the fastest ways administrators accidentally become the word you wrote earlier in the beginning of this book.

Keeping Staff and Families Informed via Newsletters and Email

Ahhh, the newsletter. Often very long, and let's be honest, not many people read them. So how do you make information more accessible to staff, students, and families?

- Send the newsletter on a consistent day and time.
- Keep the format the same so people know where to find information. For example, the weekly bell schedule is always at the top.
- A table of contents is helpful for folks who like to skim or are searching for something specific.
- Don't write long, rambling emails. Keep them short and sweet, and use bullet points often, especially for staff.
- When possible, group newsletters together, such as in a Google Drive folder, a long Google Doc, or a PDF, so they're searchable later.
- Make sure family newsletters are translated into the most common languages in your region.

- Bonus: have a little fun. I sometimes hid "Easter eggs" in emails. If students or staff spotted them, they could win a prize. It was silly, but people loved it.

Be a good listener if you want to be a good communicator. I know, blah blah blah. BUT I was a terrible multitasker. I *thought* I was good at multitasking (same with most people). Sometimes, when I was in a hurry, I tried to skim email while talking with a staff member. It was TERRIBLE. Focus on the person in front of you. Take notes. Listen more than you speak.

Speaking of Notes – Spirals

I wrote all my meeting notes with families and students in spiral notebooks. You could get them for about 25 cents during back-to-school sales. I would buy 20 or 30, give some to fellow administrators, and save others for students who needed them during the year. I wrote the start date in Sharpie on the cover, for example:

9/4/25 –

I left space to add the ending date later.

For each meeting or interview, I wrote the date at the top of a new page, took my notes, and drew a squiggly line to mark the end of the meeting.

Also know how long notes need to be kept. For Oregon, notes should be kept for 3-5 years. I'll shred mine in 2028.

A few things I wish I had done better, looking back:

- I wish I'd written more detailed notes. One time, my notes were subpoenaed, and it wasn't a major issue, but in a large or serious investigation, details matter. I documented close to everything. For example, when I made a mandatory report to our SRO, I wrote the details in my spiral even though we also completed a district form, just in case.
- I should have always written students' first and last names. I didn't always include last names because I knew the kids so well and who they associated with. When I cleaned out my office later, I found spirals with names I couldn't place at all. Not a big deal now, but what if those notes had been needed for a police investigation? Yeah. Dumb.
- Not something I didn't do better, just for your information … I didn't keep staff investigations, staff and parent notes in my student spirals. For those meetings, I used an 8.5 x 11 spiral-bound portfolio with elastic and a plastic cover. They're about $15 on Amazon. They were probably pleather, ha, and looked much fancier than my cheap school spirals and easier to spot on my desk. I usually went through one of those per year and kept district meeting notes in them as well.

3

Be Present | For Teachers, Staff, Families, and Students

I've talked a lot about being "out and about," being present in the halls, around students and staff, and making yourself available so you don't have to schedule endless office meetings. Still, some meetings are unavoidable.

I learned a great hack from Megan Jackson, an incredible first-year administrator (2022): rolling desks. Our principal purchased rolling, podium-style desks so administrators could stay visible and still access basic work during lulls. They were a little flimsy, and in hindsight, I would recommend permanent café tables and chairs placed around the school. Administrators could use them, and students could use them during lunch. Side story: we only had one lunch so many students sat in the halls to eat lunch on the dirty floor (actually, our floors were quite clean, we had an amazing custodial staff and students who had pride for our school). The café tables would have been nice. Ok squirrel! Moving on…

I stationed myself in different buildings, we had six total. Usually for students, I needed to pull for quick chats, pep talks or check-ins. This reduced time out of class for the students and allowed me to connect with teachers along the way. It was more of a pain in the ass, but it was worth it. If the rolling desks were sturdier, I would have scooted myself all over campus.

For confidential conversations, I called students in to talk in my office. If I was formally checking in using my check-in sheets, I would also use my office because oftentimes, a phone call home reporting the student's progress happened after the check-in.

Check-Ins: My FAVORITE

Check-ins require organization. I relied on my Google Calendar and, once I had one, my amazing assistant to keep me on track. Let's start with the children, as I often called the students.

The Children and Check-Ins

Checking in with students, aka the children, was a time robber, but it gave me the biggest bang for my buck and led to the most progress. It's where I really got to know them and where they got to know me. Like I said, John Ogden's nickname for me was "long talker," and sometimes he was right. I usually started my check-in list with students who had gotten into trouble. I would process the referral with them, review current grades, attendance and past behavior, and look at past grades to see if they were on track for graduation.

We set check-in schedules and goals for attendance and/or grades. Often, students need to improve in one or both areas. I checked in weekly or every other week and reported back to parents, especially when students showed improvement. I would sometimes call parents during check-in times. Students loved this because administrators usually only called when things were going badly. Parents loved it too. Sometimes we even pretended the student was in trouble just to trick parents into answering the phone.

You have to be very organized to keep check-ins running smoothly. My delightful former assistant, Jamie Netter—still a friend—handled this beautifully. She called it a "tickler." That's a real word, I looked it up. She used an index card file box organized by months and days. She placed call slips into the file based on the check-in date and how often I planned to meet with students.

In my Sterilite mobile file box, I kept hanging folders for each student I checked in with. Inside was a one-pager with small boxes where I tracked dates we met, notes about grades or attendance, and the next meeting date. Everything fit on one page, with room at the top for the student's name. Jamie kept the tickler (cringe) updated, scheduled meetings on my calendar, and radioed me if I wasn't in my office. It was awesome. See the Appendix for a link to a template.

Check-Ins With Staff

Strong relationships come first. If you're new or the staff member is new, trust takes time. Genuine interest matters. Sharing part of yourself matters too. Some ineffective administrators I worked with didn't think it was important to share aspects of their lives with staff at all. If something feels uncomfortable, then by all means, don't share it. That said, sharing yourself, your personality, your likes and dislikes, absolutely opens the door to connection.

If you use your time before and after school well and stay present in the halls, you won't need to schedule formal office check-ins very often. Still, there are times when you can't avoid them. I supervised our activities director, JD Bellum, and we needed regular weekly check-ins because of the sheer number of activities. Sometimes staff asked for regular check-ins as well, and I did my best to accommodate. When the weather allowed, I took meetings on the move—honestly, they were fantastic. Our track was centrally located and easy to access from anywhere on campus. I wish I had started walking meetings sooner instead of waiting until my last year. The only downside was note-taking, so using an app to record and transcribe notes later can help.

Check-ins are incredibly important, and again, they require organization, especially informal ones.

- Regular check-ins are easy to schedule in Google Calendar or whatever system you use.
- Reminder functions can be very helpful.
- While checking in, it's essential to be fully present. I sometimes let other work distract me during meetings, and I regret shortchanging some staff because of it.

Suggestions:

- Meet at a table without your laptop whenever possible so you can fully focus on the person in front of you. There were times when I needed my laptop, but not always.
- Take notes in your folio notebook.
- Mark action items with a circled star and boxes so action items are easy to spot. Transfer those items often to a large desk calendar. Thank you to Mike Thul and Jostens for that amazing calendar and for the smaller folio calendars each year. I loved working with Mike and his delightful wife, Karen Thul, rhymes with "cool," don't-cha-know?

- Follow up with an email to the staff member or student summarizing action items, and schedule a follow-up meeting if needed.
- Schedule calendar reminders to follow up on both your tasks and theirs.

Check-Ins With Parents

I didn't often have regular phone or in-person check-ins with parents, but there were a few. I let parents know ahead of time that there might be days when I couldn't check in at a scheduled time because school chaos happens. I always followed up by the end of the day. Parents want to know you're rooting for their student, that you see past the naughtiness, and that you want them to succeed and thrive.

I did have parents contact me sometimes daily. Again, parenting is hard and it's hard to change a child's behavior at home, especially at the high school level. One parent was texting me in the late evening or randomly asking for the bell schedule so I had to let them know to contact me through my work phone. They were ok with that.

A Fake Discipline Scenario

Wendy and Gina got into a fight during lunch in the Taco Bell parking lot. Both were suspended for three days, and our School Resource Officer (SRO) Greg Larrison spoke with each student. He explained potential charges and what could have happened, for example, disorderly conduct. By the way, I'm making all of this up.

Because there were no criminal charges, I interviewed Wendy. John Ogden was available and interviewed Gina. We wanted to see whether their stories matched. There were three witnesses, and because Wendy's and Gina's accounts differed, we sought out witnesses who appeared neutral.

Our campus security specialist went to Taco Bell to see whether he could review camera footage. Larrison also went over to see if any kids were still around who witnessed the fight. Larrison had a GREAT relationship with students. Funny thing, he had been a teacher before he became 5-O (police officer), and he had incredible rapport with kids. He was always in the halls during passing time, before school, and during lunch, including the parking lot at Safeway. We had a fantastic working relationship with Larrison. It was genuinely fun to work together during investigations.

There were things I could do that he couldn't do, and vice versa. Larrison was also funny as hell and just a great human. He kept us updated on students who got into trouble in the community. We met regularly and also met monthly with the Youth Services Team (YST), which included administrators, the SRO, probation officers, school counselors, and our licensed clinical social worker. All information shared was confidential, and the team's goal was to support students. It was a solid, effective group.

Being "out and about," visible, and available matters for staff as much as it does for students. Larrison and our campus security specialist were everywhere on campus. During lunch and passing time, administrators were also stationed in multiple locations.

Back to my fake fight. Larrison reviewed the footage, got the "real" fake story, and came back with the video on the campus security specialist's phone. He sent it to Ogden and myself. Wendy was the aggressor, but the fight was mutual, so both students received the same consequence: out-of-school suspension.

When we suspended a student, we always did the following:

- Conducted an unbiased investigation (to the best of our ability).
- Completed an out-of-school suspension (OSS) form.
- Had the student sign and date the form to indicate due process. It was rare for a student to refuse to sign. When they did sign, I reviewed the entire form again and asked whether I missed anything. Sometimes I had, so I updated it. I also let them know their signature did not admit guilt, it just indicated I went over everything on the form with them.

NOTE: each district's OSS form will differ. We were lucky and made our own form to include information we deemed important.

- Included key information on the OSS form, such as:
    - o Date of the offense
    - o Description of the offense with detailed information
    - o When and how homework could be picked up
    - o Family contact name, date, time, and phone number, or documentation of attempted contact

- Mediation date, offered or declined
- Staff informed (counselor, SpED case manager if applicable, Intervention Specialist, Athletic Director, SRO, school psychologist if applicable)
- Threat assessment and meeting date if applicable
- Trespass notice if applicable
- Expulsion hearing/Pre-expulsion meeting if applicable
- My name, email, and phone number for follow-up questions
- Due process signature and date
- Ordered homework for the student and pick-up time
- Date/time teachers were emailed for homework, unless the SRO requested to do so first.
- Reviewed grades and attendance with both the student and the parent and offered support. I also offered regular check-ins and let parents know I would follow up. This allowed me to share good news later, which parents appreciated.
- Maintained confidentiality between students. Families often wanted to know the other student's incident and/or consequences, which we couldn't share due to the Family Education Rights and Privacy Act (FERPA).
- Provided the parent with a copy of the OSS form along with my business card.

- o Homework was usually available at the end of the next day and I encouraged the student or parents to call if they did not get homework from one or more teachers.

Side note: my business cards had my personal cell number on them. I never received prank or inappropriate calls from parents or students, but I do *not* recommend doing this and took it off years later.

We offered mediation to each student and only scheduled it if both agreed. We never pressured students because mediation doesn't work unless everyone buys in. We also gave students time to think about it and decide later.

Homework was ordered for both students, and families could pick it up by the end of the following day. If a family couldn't pick it up, I offered to drop it off or email it. It was extremely important to me that students received the work they needed while suspended.

When contacting families, keep these things in mind for clear communication. Their child is not them. Treat parents with respect and dignity. If parents are angry and project that anger onto you, do your best not to take it personally. Many parents carry trauma from poor school experiences, whether from their own time in school or from what their child experienced elsewhere. Sometimes the situation is the fault of the student or parent. Pointing that out is rarely helpful. I always tried to start fresh with both the student and the family. As I've said before, I'm a long talker, and I stand by overcommunicating.

We also made sure not to "double ding" students academically while they were suspended. Our goal was to keep them caught up. We stressed to families that if they didn't hear back from a teacher about homework, they should let us know. Teachers were good about either providing assignments or giving students extra time upon return. We emailed teachers the day of a suspension, asking them to send work to the attendance office by the end of the next day. My assistant also placed notes in teacher mailboxes. Reasons for suspension were kept confidential except for counseling, administrative, and special education staff.

When first contacting a parent, especially about serious behavior, use a kind tone and be patient. Above all, remember the student is not their behavior. I always kept in mind that the kid was a good kid, or at least a good human, who made a poor choice. I explained it that way to parents. I firmly believed it then and still do.

I made plenty of poor choices in my youth, and I told both students and parents. Some parents assumed administrators were goody-two-shoes, perfect, egotistical or stuck up. Sharing a little of my own ding-dong behavior helped them relax. I did get into trouble with the 5-O at seventeen, and I still won't share what I did. I've always said, "I wasn't a bad person; I sometimes made bad decisions," and I still believe that. What I did doesn't matter. I turned out fine and believe it helped me do a better job working with students. I shared that it's less impactful if students got in trouble as minors, rather than later as adults, when consequences can follow them for life. Kids usually get it eventually. Parents don't always believe me. Boys especially take longer. That frontal cortex moves at its own damn pace.

When Calling Families Doesn't Go Well

I didn't have many truly bad parent calls. I expelled over 150 students in my twenty years as an administrator, which is a lot of hard conversations. I probably hung up on fewer than three parents total. Fewer than ten parents yelled to the point that I had to end the call. Parents did yell at me, but I could usually de-escalate the situation.

I don't tolerate parents yelling at staff. That's an absolute hells-to-the-no. I told staff they could hang up if a parent was yelling or say they couldn't continue the conversation and would call back when the parent was calm. I was fine with them hanging up and documenting what happened via email or looping in an administrator.

For yelly parents, let them vent. Their child may already be difficult at home, and your call is often the icing on the cake. It helps if you've already built rapport through earlier conversations about smaller issues. I gave parents my full attention and a lot of empathy and listening time. Parenting is hard. It's critical not to tie a child's behavior to the worth of either the child or the parent. Above all, don't take what parents or kids say personally. It isn't about you. It's about their child.

Evaluation and Observations | Processes

I was formally observed exactly one time when I was a teacher. ONE time in twelve years. I was a good teacher, but imagine how much better I could have been with regular feedback. I might have been a master teacher. When I became an administrator, I made observations and feedback a priority.

That said, I had years when I could have majorly improved overall in this. Totally owning that. It took time to organize myself around this instructional leadership piece, which is honestly the most amazing and fun part of the job. There were a few systems we used to support teachers and staff through evaluation.

Goals

We created a goals bank in a Google Sheet and had teachers add to it. We divided goals into categories like SEL, math, literacy, communication, and more. Teachers could select from the bank or create their own. We encouraged teachers to choose shared goals so they could collaborate. We also asked them to choose goals they were already working on.

Teachers are always trying to improve, at least 98 percent of them. Let's be honest, goal setting is a hoop they have to jump through, so we might as well make it useful and relevant. I also helped teachers who had specific areas to improve, and this applied to classified staff as well.

Classified Staff

In my past district, classified staff were formally evaluated every other year but to submit goals yearly. The process I used for classified staff is working with teachers who have frequent contact with classified employees (ex: paraprofessionals working in classrooms). I would gather feedback and observations from the teachers. If there were issues, I observed in the classrooms myself. At the end of the school year, I met with each classified staff member and went over their goal and also did goal setting for the next school year. This made the process smoother for the following year.

Teachers

Teachers are busy. Every fall, I set goal-setting meetings and let teachers reschedule if needed (they rarely did)—so much easier for them. I created a Google Sheet with tabs for probationary teachers, contract teachers, and classified staff. In my former district, teachers selected two student learning and growth goals and one professional goal. Contract teachers were evaluated every other year, while probationary teachers were evaluated annually for three years.

See Appendix for a link to an example and template.

The sheet included columns for:

- Staff name
- Department
- Teacher status (P1, P2, P3, C)
- License expiration date
- Completion tracking, including:
- Goal-setting meeting
- SLG 1 completed
- SLG 2 completed
- Professional goal completed
- Self-assessment completed
- Informal observation dates
- Formal observation date
- Required documents, such as pre-observation meeting and form, post-observation meeting, and reflection dates
- Mid-year review and reflection dates
- End-of-year reflection date
- Summative evaluation date
- Any other required items

My assistant tracked these items and helped manage my calendar for observations. We reviewed everything during our weekly meetings. It was a lifesaver.

Informal Observations

For informal observations, I typically scheduled about nine per week, three per day, at different times. For example, early morning, mid-period, end of period, or end of day. I usually observed three times a week in one-hour blocks, observing three teachers. Because observations capture only a moment in time, I also did frequent walkthroughs beyond required observations.

The three classrooms I observed were always close together. I used either a clipboard and paper, because I'm old, or the iWalk Observation app on my iPad, which I loved. It was designed by a teacher, and the support was outstanding. I wish I had learned all its features. I could take photos of students, classrooms, and teachers, and send observations with feedback directly to teachers' email right away.

I usually completed write-ups immediately after the trio of observations or at the end of the day, once students and staff had left. That made it much easier to remember the lesson accurately.

When informal observations were on my calendar, I sent a group email letting teachers know I would go into classrooms that week. I also asked if there were days or periods I should avoid. Teachers appreciated this, and it kept me accountable. Pro tip for administrators reading this book: Douglas Reeves suggested telling teachers things like, "Today I'll be looking for checks for understanding" or "Today I'll be looking for 100% engagement." It turns observations into a team challenge; how can we get to 100% together, not a gotcha?

Our district used the Danielson Framework for evaluation. I'm not a fan. The language makes "distinguished" extremely difficult to achieve. As a concrete thinker and former math teacher, phrases like "all students" drove me nuts. All students are unrealistic.

When giving feedback, I intentionally referenced evaluation components. For example, Danielson Component 1c, setting instructional outcomes, under Domain 1. I had referenced this in formal observations when appropriate. In informal observations, which were usually 15 to 20 minutes, I focused on Domain 2, Classroom Environment, and Domain 3, Instruction. I didn't reference Domain 1 or Domain 4 in informal observations for obvious reasons.

Sometimes a lesson didn't go well. It happened. Observations are stressful no matter how supportive you try to make them. If a lesson went sideways, I offered a do-over. Who cares? It's a moment in time. The goal is useful feedback that helps a teacher improve. Teachers appreciated this.

Gathering Data for Teachers

I also gathered data for teachers. For example, if a teacher complained about a particularly tough class right after lunch, a notoriously squirrely time, I would offer the following:

- Gather data and give feedback on the class.
- Offer to speak with students in an unofficial capacity, usually pulling five to eight students for an informal, helpful "stop being a butthead" conversation. This was very effective.

Often, when I met with students, it was a quick process. I asked what was going on, how they could be part of fixing the situation, and I always dug into attendance and grades. Sometimes we had to problem-solve. I was also getting to know ding-dong students without them formally getting in trouble, and I didn't call home after these chats. If a regular check-in led to the conversation, we set a few goals. After a successful check-in, the student and I would call their parents together. Win, win, WIN.

Formal Observations

I used a template email that went out to teachers with links to all required forms and a request for a few dates or periods that worked best for them. Teachers usually responded quickly, either to me or my assistant. The district required a pre-observation form, lesson plan, and post-observation form, along with pre- and post-observation conferences.

The pre-observation conference was a ten- to fifteen-minute meeting. I didn't hold the conference if forms or the lesson plan weren't submitted or brought to the meeting. I was strict about that because we needed those materials to have a meaningful conversation. If they weren't ready, the observation was rescheduled. This happened only a handful of times.

Items I requested for these meetings:

- Pre- or post-observation form with reflection completed
- Lesson plan, not overly detailed, but including transitions and standards covered

- Seating chart and list of students with IEPs, TAG, 504s, ELL, or migrant status

End-of-Year Summative Evaluation

My best advice for end-of-year summative evaluations is simple:

- Review the teacher's self-assessment early in the year and be realistic with them. Occasionally, average–or below-average–teachers rated themselves as "distinguished" in every category. I addressed this with humor. I once laughed and said, "Really?!" The teacher would laugh too. We both knew it was bullshit.

- Do *not* go through every domain and component one by one with scores. Don't do it. It invites tit-for-tat debates and drags meetings out unnecessarily. Evaluation scores don't really go anywhere anyway—unless maybe a teacher is fired, and even then, probably not.

- Instead, highlight three or four areas the teacher did exceptionally well and a few areas for growth. Add detail. Use this as a springboard for discussion and planning for the next school year.

- Observe classrooms more than the minimum required. Walkthroughs matter.

Short Shot Walkthroughs

I loved the "Short Shot" walkthrough form another administrator shared with me. I can't remember who it was, maybe Sam Thompson. He was such a kind and funny person. It would have been fun to work in the same building with him.

The "Short Shot" was a simple half-sheet where I would observe a classroom for about ten minutes and write down observations from that short "moment in time." Positive observations went under *Noticings*, and questions or concerns went under *Wonderings.* I often included verbatim notes and timestamps. If what I observed aligned with Charlotte Danielson's Framework Domain 2 (Classroom Environment) or Domain 3 (Instruction), I noted the specific domain and component.

I would leave the sheet somewhere the teacher would find it later. Teachers appreciated receiving short, specific feedback from walkthrough visits.

When writing summative evaluations at the end of the year, I used these notes to provide specific, concrete feedback—for example, 2a: Creating an Environment of Respect and Rapport. If I observed something strong, I referenced the component and described what I saw. This made summative evaluations much easier and backed by "evidence" from past observations.

I focused only on Classroom Environment and Instruction because it was difficult to give meaningful feedback on Planning and Preparation or Professional Responsibilities during a short walkthrough. Teachers responded positively to the short shot feedback.

That said, I fell short year after year on the number of short shots I completed. When the district moved to an online observation system, I stopped doing them during my last few years as an administrator. I should have kept them up and done a better job of getting into classrooms daily. As a teacher, I was observed and given feedback once. Over twelve years, I was told I was a good teacher, but I could have been a great teacher with consistent guidance, feedback, and collaboration. That would have benefited me and, more importantly, my students.

To evaluate effectively, administrators must be present in classrooms and provide relevant feedback. Informal observations often fell by the wayside because of the constant emergencies that come with administration. Formal observations always happened, but keeping up with informal ones was a struggle until I had an assistant. What the?!!!

5

Trust Your People | Don't Micromanage

Being an administrator is an IMPOSSIBLE job. Long hours. Little praise. People don't understand what you do every day. It's complex, time-consuming, and sometimes heartbreaking. No one cares if your job is hard. Period. And that's ok!

Micromanaging is a 100 percent don't-do. You'll never earn trust or respect if you micromanage. Trusting others is scary, but I've worked under both types of administrators: micromanagers and those who empower staff. The difference is night and day.

Administrators are busy. We don't have time to know everything. It's impossible, even in schools with multiple administrators. At my former school, we had four administrators and had to trust staff to do the right thing. Could things go wrong? Yes. But for your sanity, empowerment is necessary.

When I worked under micromanagers, communication was slow and unclear. All administrators had to attend nearly every meeting. I was required to meet multiple times a month just to plan presentations. Every decision had to go through them. It was exhausting, unprofessional, and honestly ridiculous. It's no surprise that research shows this kind of meeting overload is harmful—*The Surprising Science of Meetings* by Steven G. Rogelberg explains how poorly run meetings don't just waste time; they drain energy, lower morale, and make people feel like their time doesn't matter. His book is full of practical ways to make meetings efficient, purposeful, and actually worth attending.

If something goes wrong, the administrator takes the blame. That's the job. If something goes well, give credit to the person responsible. That builds trust. In twenty years, very few things went wrong. Most people want to do a good job. Assuming best intent matters.

Success builds on success. Our job is to trust, promote, and encourage staff to grow beyond what they think they can. Of course, if you have a fabulous teacher, you want to keep them at your school. However, if that teacher would be an incredible administrator, it's your job to promote them to the next level, as long as it's what they want. Never tell a teacher they'd make a great administrator if you don't mean it.

Administrators are the face of the school and district. As instructional leaders, you're the driving force of your school. If there are multiple administrators, everyone must be aligned. Disagree behind closed doors. Present a united front publicly.

What administrators should do, in general:

- Keep your office door open whenever possible.
- Avoid bias. Favoritism is obvious and destroys culture.

- Be fair and consistent with everyone.
- Be in the halls during passing time. Don't schedule meetings that run into it.
- Be cheerful and positive with staff.
- Don't answer "How are you?" with "busy." Everyone is busy. No one cares if you are busy, for fucks sake.
- Show appreciation and celebrate staff. See the chapter about fun in the workplace.
- Communicate clearly and respond within 24 to 48 hours. If you don't have an answer, say so and follow up.
- Handle email before and after school, not during. With parents, overcommunicate. Always remember to contact both parents when appropriate.

Together

We are all in this together. Education is hard. Teachers work beyond contracted hours, spend their own money, and give everything they have. They deserve respect and trust.

Self-efficacy is KEY. We must believe our staff can do their jobs. For me, that means:

- Being open to new ideas
- Listening more
- Not interrupting

Is this hard? Yes. We're busy. We have shit to do. But slowing down and giving people space to speak builds trust faster than you think. Education is a "we" job. No one is more important than anyone else, except maybe the students. Everyone matters. Assume best intent. Always.

6

Fun in the Workplace | Celebration

Hell yes. LET'S GOOOOO!

This is the chapter to pay attention to. Being an educator is hard, especially now. COVID nearly broke the system. At the same time, schools were asked to shift toward restorative practices and reduce suspensions. I support restorative justice, but without dedicated staff to manage the process (and do it right), it can be extremely difficult to implement effectively.

Okay, that was a bit of an unintentional rabbit hole, haha. Let's talk about fun and why it's ESSENTIAL for school staff.

Education is tough. There's very little fanfare or recognition. I've always been a silly, goofy person. Strict, so I've been told, but fair and fun, if that makes sense. Even before COVID, I implemented ways to celebrate staff. Some people didn't like it at first, but over time, most got on board.

Fun and celebration matter because people are worn down. It's easy to jump on the complainer bandwagon. Having fun and celebrating gives people a positive outlet and is a GREAT way to retain staff. When people feel happy and valued, they're more likely to stay. It also shows staff that you care about them as people, not just employees. That kind of care is gold.

There's actual research behind this, too—Vivek Murthy, in *Together,* talks about how loneliness shows up at work. So if your staff feels disconnected and drained, it's not just them being negative—it's a culture issue.

I genuinely cared about every person I worked with. Okay, a few drove me a little nuts, but they still had good in them and were doing their best, for the most part. Caring can't be faked. Take the time to get to know your staff, students, and families. Kids, especially, can spot BS instantly. Lead with as little bias as possible and assume best intent.

After I retired, I still volunteered at the school where I'd worked a few hours per week. I would run into staff I knew often. Almost every time, they told me how much I was missed. It led me to reflect on the significant impact administrators have on school culture, whether positive or negative. Now I am a silly goose. I'm not for everyone. I can be a lot for people, energetic and sometimes too enthusiastic. Hopefully a few staff I used to work with read this and text me yay or nay. Haha! My heart is in the right place and staff let me know they appreciated my efforts and fun. Staff seeing their admin having fun and showing "the love" is a part of trust building. Some of the things we did took little effort, but were oh so great. Anyway, here are some ideas you can implement in your school too.

Sunshine Committee

We had Sunshine Committees in both high schools where I served as an administrator. Participation was optional, and staff donations were strictly voluntary. The suggested donation amount was $10 per person. To incentivize donations, I offered raffle tickets using the following structure: one ticket for a $10 donation and one additional ticket for every extra $5 donated.

A few days after payday (around the end of September), I picked a winner and covered one class period for that person. It used to be half a day, but things were sometimes too crazy for me to miss that much time. I set an expiration date sometime before winter break and would not cover the day before Thanksgiving Break, Winter Break, Friday the 13th, or full moon days. Yes, that's legit. Friday the 13th and full moon days are consistently more rambunctious and require more discipline. We had a number of activities we organized for staff…

Fun Ideas We Implemented

Happy Hour Events

These were sometimes called POETS meetings (Piss Off Everyone, Tomorrow Is Saturday), Cookies and Milk, or simply First Fridays. First Fridays made it easy to remember to meet on the first Friday of each month. The Sunshine Committee paid for a few appetizers. If I attended as an administrator, I might buy an appetizer and leave after about 30 minutes. Let's be honest, no matter how much people like you, they don't really want their boss there. Facts. Some staff organized happy hours at a local winery owned by one of our teachers, which was especially fun.

Guess the Candy in the Jar

We filled a jar with seasonal candy and had the staff guess how many pieces were inside. Guesses were submitted on paper and placed in a locked box. The jar went to the closest guess without going over. We made sure the jar couldn't be opened because there were a few cheaters on staff. Sometimes we hid large candy bars in the middle to make the guessing harder, which was a little evil but effective. Sorry to my mathie colleagues…

Staff Summer Slideshow

I emailed out a Google slideshow template with an example slide as a guide and several blank slides. Each staff member added their own slide with photos of family, activities, pets, and summer highlights. The email went out about a month before preservice. We played the slideshow on a loop with music as staff arrived.

Hallway Bowling on Grade Day

One teacher owned a plastic bowling set. We set it up in the main hallway and announced it over the intercom. We advertised it ahead of time in the weekly staff newsletter. It was genuinely fun watching people mingle and laugh.

In-Service Pancake Breakfast

Mark Martens, one of our former athletic directors and all around great guy, had an excellent homemade pancake and syrup recipe. The admin team cooked pancakes and sausage on the in-service day after winter break. We brought electric griddles, arrived around 6 a.m., and served breakfast to teachers. The Sunshine Committee provided ingredients, coffee, and creamer. It made the staff feel appreciated, it was a lot of fun and it was delicious.

Minute to Win It Staff Games

We ran a few of these before staff meetings or professional development sessions. Staff competed by department, with smaller departments combined as needed. We learned that keeping it small worked best. When we tried to scale it up for the entire year, it flopped because of how much time it took to organize teams, points, etc.

Crock Pot Wars

This was a staff favorite. Usually held in November, staff brought crock pot dishes in categories such as entrée, side, and dessert. Staff sampled items and teachers voted during lunch, and classified staff voted between ten a.m. and two p.m. Our Career Technical Education program created plaques and added winners each year. We coordinated with the district electrician to ensure outlets could safely handle the load. Staff signed up anonymously by number. My assistant, Jamie Netter, won every year. Her secret was jalapeños. The Sunshine Committee provided supplies, and participation was optional. Everyone was welcome to enjoy the delicious food, whether or not they brought something to share.

Salsa Competition

Held a few times in the spring, usually May. Fun, competitive, food-focused and quite delicious. I later learned garden vegetables weren't quite ready yet. I'm a black thumb. A suggestion is to let staff know we were having this competition at the end of the school year so they could plant their salsa gardens that summer.

Fun Giveaways

Occasional small giveaways for things like inspirational quotes or staff tips. The most popular item was a toilet bowl light. I never found them again for the $2 price tag.

Secret Santa

Participants completed a form with favorite items and preferences. Spending was capped at $25. Small daily gifts were encouraged the week before winter break. The final reveal included treats provided by the Sunshine Committee. If there was an odd number of participants, the organizer served as the extra Secret Santa. For clever ideas for Secret Santa forms, check out Canva.

Gifts

We gave gifts for a few main events for staff:

- Retirement – a handmade sign with the staff member's last name (made by a staff member) and a gift card ($50)
- Death or illness – a succulent plant, grown by our horticulture students
- New baby – a handmade baby bowl with the baby's name in the bottom, around $10
- Illness – we gave departments cards to give if needed for folks in their department

- Goodbye – a card with a $10 – $20 gift card, if a staff member was moving on to another job (this fluctuated, based on how much money we had in our kitty)

I spoke to my past colleague Theresa Kahl about our Sunshine giveaways and she remembered she won a free period and an egg cooker (said with a smile) – people matter and remember kindness. She retired a few years ago … such a dedicated teacher, she loved the kids so much!

Staff Kudos

It is worth its weight in gold to celebrate your staff. It takes time and planning, but it helps with overall staff well-being and retention.

Hump Day Bump

This was a weekly, staff-to-staff kudos email sent every Wednesday. I collected submissions via Google Form sent out Friday or Monday prior. Wednesday mornings, I compiled the email with names and kudos, corrected typos, and added quotes, jokes, or memes.

After five years, we had over 6,000 kudos. I chose not to share sender names to keep the focus on appreciation rather than credit. Noah Megowan submitted the most kudos by far–such a joyous, kind and energetic person!.

For example:

Anna Nguyen – You approach each day and each person with a smile – thank you for the impact you make on our students and school community!

Alex Frixione – You're always thoughtful and real. Great person to go to for insight.

Guess what? These HDBs were given to these two amazing educators … I sure miss them and their amazingness!

Staff Shout Outs

Similar to Hump Day Bump, but kudos came from students and parents. I included the google form link in a weekly newsletter to parents. I would alternate sending the form to parents and students. I edited submissions for appropriateness and clarity. Occasionally, I called students in to clarify inside jokes. The messages consistently reflected deep appreciation for staff.

Staff Pet Slideshow

Another Google slideshow where staff added photos of their pets. We shared it at a staff meeting and ran it before the meeting started. I also included it in the Hump Day Bump or staff newsletter.

Lottery Fun

Perhaps I did this … or not. It's probably best if you check the rules in your school.

When the lottery climbed over $300 million, I sent an email inviting staff to join in the fun of buying tickets as a group. They had until the end of the day to drop their money in a large manila envelope on the meeting table in my office and write their name on it.

I snapped photos of the envelope with all the names and the tickets and emailed them to the participants so everyone could watch the drawing.

It was fun imagining what we'd all do if we won—and joking about the scandal it would cause if the entire staff quit at the same time.

Honestly, we were all a little disappointed the next morning when we had to come back to work.

Graduation Notes for Staff from Seniors

Seniors wrote appreciation notes to one K-12 staff member and a graduation ticket was provided by the school. Notes were distributed (through courier or mailed) across the district, including to retired staff. I read every note and followed up when clarification was needed. Sometimes "inside jokes" were not clear, so I called in the students to check. More often than not, it was legit.

Grad March

In the fall, I worked with transportation to organize a field trip, busing seniors to elementary schools (they chose which bus to ride) and then to middle schools. This happened around 3-4 weeks before graduation. Because the spring is a busy time for elementary field trips, we had to plan early. Transportation did us a solid by blocking out the whole day for us so we were the only field trip in the district.

Graduates visited their former elementary and middle schools in cap and gown, right after the mandatory Senior Meeting. Graduates received the dos and don'ts of graduation, finishing strong, appropriate behavior and also got their cap and gowns at the end of the meeting. We also told them to NOT wear their tassels, they were easily lost.

Teachers and elementary/middle school students lined the halls and celebrated the graduates. It was powerful for everyone involved. We gave each school the approximate time of arrival and they organized whatever celebration they wanted. It was so fun witnessing everyone's joy and listening to past teachers recognize past students. It was such a special K-12 celebration.

7

New Teachers | Keep 'em at Our School

One of our biggest priorities as administrators was supporting and retaining new teachers. For many years, our school built our own support system because district support was limited. During the last five years of my administrative career, the district finally created a formal program to help new teachers, and it improved over time. One funny story: the district put on their first new teacher half-day training about how to write sub plans. What the heck?! Cracked me the up! Over the years, the district support improved for new teachers.

Our school would pay new teachers to come in the day or so before the first day for all teachers. At our first new teacher support meeting, we would do the following for new teachers:

- Welcome gift ideas
    - colorful paper clips
    - a staple remover, fun Post-its
    - Ticonderoga pencils (the good ones)
    - gel pens and highlighter pens
    - travel Tylenol
    - a variety of fun size candy bars

- school swag
- a good stapler
- adult scissors, etc.

NOTE: We would touch base with department leaders to see if they had adequate supplies in their room and purchase accordingly.

- Tour of the school (by admin or department leader)
- New Staff Handbook (updated each year and we'd go over parts of it with teachers). This was also available to all staff online.
- Introduction to key staff, admin, and DLs in departments with new teachers (if available)
- Technology support
- Question and answer session

More Ideas that Make a Difference

A few weeks later, we would put on a luncheon for new first and second year teachers, union leadership, administrative staff, and administrators. We often invited the union president, bookkeeper, registrar, head counselor, administrative assistants, and other administrators. It was voluntary, and we would feed everyone invited. Teachers could chat with each other, ask the group questions, etc. Second-year teachers were especially helpful because they had just survived year one and could give very practical advice and great tips to the newbies. Those conversations helped new teachers realize they were not the only ones feeling overwhelmed.

Throughout the year we offered a mix of optional support opportunities (note the word *optional*):

- Informal lunches (byol)
- Short, after-school help sessions (entering grades, progress reports, union questions, student management, technology training, etc.)
- Supervisor and department leader check-ins

Other ideas I learned about later included:

- Positive notes at the end of each school day the first week
- End of week check-in with supervisor (Thursday, not Friday)

Make sure new teachers have the technology they need a few weeks before the preservice PD (if possible). Technology is a teacher's lifeline! We made sure technology staff were available for new teacher questions and training.

Best Practices from a COSA Workshop

Later in my career, I presented a session on supporting new teachers with our HR director and another principal at the Coalition of School Administrators (COSA) Assistant Principal Conference in 2019. During the session, administrators shared ideas during roundtable discussions. Here are some of the best suggestions.

Best Support Ideas from the Workshop:

- Time in classroom, direct feedback, and mentoring from a supervisor
- End-of-day daily debriefs with mentor teacher for the first few weeks
- The mentor is a confidential, non-evaluative sounding board
- Time with colleagues away from students to vent, share, etc.
- Specific orientation or training for new teachers before other teachers
- Monthly meetings
- School culture pieces, like staff T-shirts
- Staff gear. Do *not* make them pay for the items
- First day of school: deliver their favorite morning drink
- End of day: bring them their favorite candy or snack
- If your school reads a yearly book, share last year's yearbook, so the new teacher can gain familiarity
- Do *not* invite them to be on committees yet

District-Level Support that Helps New Teachers

- Welcoming environment
- One-on-one support for new hire paperwork
- Paid professional development (PD) before other teachers. For some districts, PD funds are first-come, first-served and those funds run out at the end of the school year.
- Onboarding supervisor resource guide
- All Staff Welcome and PD day
- Monthly staff newsletter
- Mentors for new teachers
- PD: setting up positive classrooms, differentiation, etc.
- Teacher on Special Assignment (TOSA): mentor, behavior and inclusion specialist
- Wellness Program and Employee Assistance Program (EAP)

During their first year, new teachers are completely overwhelmed, usually with no complaints (imagine the brave face of someone suffering). Small acts of encouragement and support can make the difference between someone staying at your school or leaving teaching altogether. It is not our responsibility as administrators to fix every issue new teachers have, we can make sure they know they are not alone.

Many of these ideas are small, but they go a long way in helping new teachers feel supported during a very overwhelming first year.

8

Self-Care | Social Emotional Learning

My focus has always been on relationships, even before the Social Emotional Learning (SEL) push during and after COVID. Our school has had a licensed clinical social worker for over twenty-five years serving both students and staff. We believe it's essential to care for people as whole humans, not just employees or students.

Sometimes people don't realize they need TLC or how powerful it can be. I want to go a little deeper into my month off for mental health. I called it my month of repose. I wasn't sleeping and lived in a constant state of anxiety. I'm not an anxious person, so it was alarming. I contacted my doctor, went on medication, and took a month off using FMLA and sick time. I had nine months available. I started feeling better after about two weeks, but my doctor encouraged me to take the full month for the medication to work. I returned after a month and was open about why I had been out. Mental health is something people generally don't talk about. Of course, people speculated, and they were careful not to ask. I told them flat out, just as I would have if I had been out for a physical medical reason. They were surprised that I shared my mental wellness reason. Let's stop stigmatizing mental health and do a better job taking care of ourselves.

Self-care is something educators do a terrible job with. Being an educator now is very different from being an educator pre-COVID. That was a little over six years ago. I admit I didn't protect my peace well. I worked too much. My days were twelve to sixteen hours long, plus at least one weekend day. That's absurd. No wonder I fizzled out mentally. My advice to new administrators is to set boundaries and maintain a reasonable work-life balance. I can't give time back to my kids or my husband. He was essentially a single dad. I'm sorry for that and can't undo it. I have to move forward and let that go.

One way I tried to protect my peace was by not bringing work home. Home was my haven. If I had work to do, I did it at work, which explains my long hours. During my last six years as an administrator, I lived and worked in the same town, which helped. If I had supervision duty, I stayed at work. I didn't go home first. Once I was home, it was too hard to leave again. So take care of yourself, protect your peace, and don't live to work. Maybe I would have lasted longer if I had done a better job of this, but I'm not sorry I'm retired. Ha.

I also should have accepted much earlier that my inbox was never going to be empty. It's okay to leave things until the next day. The things I never left were:

- Contacting parents regarding discipline, student check-ins, or phone messages
- Student management issues or mandatory reports, which in my state must be filed within twenty-four hours
- A final end-of-day scan of emails and phone messages

Organizations move on.

They can function without you.

I know that now.

As a Leader Taking Care of Your Staff

Shit runs downhill, and you know I'm right. If there are issues in your school, it isn't the fault of teachers or staff. It's on administration. It takes a special kind of crazy to be an administrator and a middle school teacher. People aren't going to thank you. That's a given. But it's incredible when you make a connection with a student, parent, or staff member and watch it grow over the years. At the high school level, you get four years with students. That matters.

For some administrators, ego gets in the way. I don't understand that. No one is better than anyone else. Storytime. When I was little, my mom was a lunch lady at an elementary school and later a library media assistant, both classified positions. She taught my brother and me that no one is better than anyone else. Good people jump in and do hard work. No one is above any job.

She was sometimes treated poorly because she was a classified employee. She was also discriminated against because of her skin color, something I witnessed repeatedly.

Ego can drive people to treat others like shit. Too much weight is often placed on what someone does for a living or how they look. My mom is incredible. She majored in chemistry and math in college in 1957, when very few women did. She worked as a chemist for the U.S. Food and Drug Administration in San Francisco before marrying my dad and staying home during our early years. When we were in middle school, she returned to work in an elementary school after years of volunteering.

She is the kindest, most joyful person I know, and I strive to be like her. I learned invaluable lessons about character and how to treat people well, unlike how my mom was sometimes treated.

Remember the word you wrote down at the beginning of this book? Some administrators become that word because they feel overwhelmed, isolated and try to solve every problem themselves – not because they *want* to be a _________.

It's important to have high expectations for others and for yourself, while also not sweating the small stuff. That balance took me time to learn.

Some things I focused on, and yes, they're easier said than done:

- Trust your people. People want to do a good job. You can't do everything, so delegation is necessary and builds capacity.
- Assume best intent. See above.
- Follow the contract. Always. It's required and shows respect for staff.
- Do not nitpick. Things don't need to be done exactly your way.

- Strive to be unbiased. Look beyond personality, and find the good in everyone.
- Be culturally competent – learn about others, have humility, be self-aware and learn about your own bias
- Believe in your people, including the snarky ones. There's something good in every single person.
- Be a worker bee. Jump in and do whatever needs to be done. Yes, I cleaned up poop more than once.
- Praise often and be specific. This profession doesn't offer much external validation. Celebrate your people.
- Help others. Teachers are busy. Sending a link they could technically find themselves still matters.
- Take time to build relationships. Be genuine. Don't fake it.
- Don't micromanage. It's insulting and questions intelligence and integrity. If things go well, give credit. If they go poorly, take the blame. Welcome to leadership.
- Admit when you're wrong. With staff, parents, and students. It shows strength and humanity.
- Communicate early and often. Overcommunication helped me navigate difficult, litigious discipline situations without lawyers or media involvement.
- Care about your people. Teaching now is very different from teaching pre-COVID. Keep that front and center.

- Work to live, not the other way around. Everyone is replaceable.
- Promote your staff. Encourage growth and advancement when earned and desired, even when it's a loss for your school.
- Gather feedback only if you plan to use it.
- Take care of yourself. This was my weakest area.

Feedback and Classroom Presence

How many times have you been asked to give feedback only to have it ignored or used against you? As a teacher and administrator, that wasn't my experience, and I may have been lucky. When I worked as a TOSA for a year and a half, I saw a very different reality. Surveys went out regularly. I mentored ten of seventeen new teachers and encouraged them to be honest if they wanted change. That was always my view of surveys.

As an administrator, we sent surveys a few times a year, gathered feedback, and used it to make decisions. In my TOSA role, that wasn't what staff experienced. People believed they faced retribution for honest feedback. With only seventeen teachers total, they felt administrators could identify respondents based on how questions were structured. It was deeply disheartening. I gave honest feedback consistently and never saw change or even acknowledgment. Often my feedback mirrored others', so it wasn't isolated.

The admin teams I worked on were transparent about decision-making. We generally did one of three things:

- Gathered feedback and made a decision based on the majority or department leader majority
- Gathered feedback, considered it carefully, and made an informed decision
- Did not gather feedback and made the decision outright

Not every decision is democratic, and not every decision requires input. Staff appreciated knowing when decisions were simply made for them. When feedback did drive decisions, we shared the results. It is crucial to value your staff's time and effort by being honest about when feedback will—and will not—shape the outcome.

Developing Leadership in Staff

We held regular meetings with department leaders. They were self-nominated or by department members, and the admin team interviewed them for the role. A nomination alone didn't mean a teacher had the qualifications. Each DL received a stipend for leadership duties. We needed to trust DLs to share information accurately with their departments. Once a decision was made, even if a DL disagreed, they supported it publicly. We operated as a united front.

Encouraging leadership in staff is critical. Sometimes even struggling staff rise to the occasion when given responsibility. It's tempting to keep a fantastic teacher who volunteers, leads PD, and carries a heavy load, but the best move is to encourage growth beyond your building. Not every teacher wants to be an administrator, but strong administrators matter. I didn't believe every teacher should go into administration, but some have the qualities to positively impact far more students, families, and schools in that role. Majalise Tolan's and Rachael George's *She Leads* shows exactly how women in education can step up, own their leadership, and make a real difference. It's full of practical advice, real stories, and encouragement that reminds us leadership isn't about titles—it's about influence, impact, and having the guts to push yourself and others to grow. Her book reinforced what I saw in my own mentors: that nurturing potential in the right people pays off in ways you can't even measure.

I was encouraged early to pursue administration. I would not call myself a rockstar, but I worked hard, followed through, communicated clearly, upheld standards, and focused on relationships. I had memorable mentors along the way. Sam Scott, a retired administrator in Oregon, was the first administrator I worked with. He was kind, loved kids, and made tough decisions with humanity. Glen Rutherford, my principal at the time, finally pushed me into administration. He was supportive, encouraging, and led with an open-door policy. I trusted him completely.

Receiving Feedback and Handling Conflict

Another note on feedback is being open to receiving it yourself. When things don't go well, learn from it. Don't beat yourself up, but take criticism with grace. Administrators expect staff to grow from feedback, and administrators must do the same. Ego has no place here. This work is about students and the school, not about you.

Everyone makes mistakes. It's infuriating not to be listened to, especially when taking a risk by speaking up. Often, people want to be heard more than they want to be right. Don't take things personally. There's a lot of emotion from staff, students, and families. Most of the time, it isn't about you. Unless you're being a jerk.

You'll be wrong sometimes. That's normal. Admit it, learn from it, and move on. We talk all the time about modeling the behavior we expect, and that includes owning mistakes and apologizing. If that's hard for you, administration will be rough.

I once supervised the English department. I was a math teacher. At our first meeting, I apologized in advance because Language Arts wasn't my area of expertise. They were gracious and taught me along the way. I asked questions and learned a great deal.

I worked hard not to take things personally. It isn't easy, but becoming a safe person for others to express feelings and concerns pays off. Sometimes people cross lines, but many times parents are upset and just trying to be heard.

They often just needed to vent. I'm not saying you have to tolerate abuse, but patience, asking questions, and giving people space to express themselves matters. In twenty years, I received exactly one semi-threatening voicemail, and it was from a drunk student. I hung up on fewer than half a dozen parents because they were completely out of control. I was always clear with staff that it's absolutely okay to end a call if someone is being excessively rude or obnoxious. People are braver behind keyboards and phones. Many times, I was warned that a parent was irate before a meeting, only to have the conversation go just fine. I think that happened because the meeting was face-to-face.

Families and Trauma Awareness

A side note on irate parents and students. In my experience, some of the most rambunctious and angry parents weren't treated well when they were in school or when their children were in previous schools. This isn't research-based, just observation. I made a point to treat families with respect and to take the time to listen and get to know them. Their students weren't "bad" people, and I made sure families knew that. The behavior was the issue, not the child. Parents are *not* their children.

That doesn't mean parents were blameless. I often didn't know what was really happening in a household. Sometimes families lacked resources, and I did what I could to help. I was called a "long talker," and that was true. It was worth it every time. One parent once told me she appreciated that I always treated her with respect. She had been treated poorly by administrators and teachers in the past. Her child was a handful, but she was doing her best.

Some families live with low socioeconomic status, and that can persist for generations. Too often, that comes with poor treatment from others, including educators. I valued how much parents knew about their children. They knew them best. Did some parents enable their kids? Yes. Parenting is hard, and some struggled with boundaries, so they asked for my input, especially around discipline.

I built strong relationships with parents through regular student check-ins. I shared updates with families and often enjoyed "strategizing" with both parents and students. I gathered background information and experiences from both. My focus wasn't primarily behavioral. I checked in with students about how they were doing at their job of school, attendance, grades, and behavior. Most struggled first with attendance or academics, and behavior followed.

The Magic Bullet

You already know this. It's relationships, real relationships. Everything here is based on my experience and feedback from staff, students, and families. I cared deeply about the people I worked with and for. I wanted them to succeed. They knew my heart, my flaws, and why I was in education. I'm not profound, and I'm of average intelligence, but I believe deeply in the power of people. I choose to believe in the good in others. We all stumble. We help each other back up. That's the magic.

So ... Don't be That Administrator

Closing Message

Leadership in schools is challenging. You'll make difficult decisions. You'll make mistakes (uh guaranteed!). Along the way, you'll learn that small choices shape the kind of leader you become.

There will be days when you get it right and days when you wish you had a do-over. The most important thing is to never stop learning, listening and remembering what it feels like to "stand in the light," just like the people you lead (and Yoda).

Leadership isn't about being perfect. It's about being intentional.

Remember the word you wrote on the first page.

Don't let that word be **YOU.**

If this guide was helpful, pass it on. Merçi!

Proof That it's Not Just Me

Books That Back It Up

If you're the kind of person who likes a little research, a little perspective, or just wants to go deeper into this work, here are a few books worth your time.

Some of these will validate what you're already thinking.

Some might challenge you a bit.

All of them, in one way or another, reinforce this idea: people matter more than programs.

Leadership & Culture

Lead It Like Lasso: A Leadership Book for Life. Your Life.
— Marnie Stockman, Ed. D. and Nick Coniglio

A practical (and genuinely refreshing) look at what people-first leadership looks like in real life. It shows that kindness, trust, and consistency aren't just nice ideas—they're what actually make people feel valued and want to stay.

Fearless Schools: Building Trust and Resilience for Learning, Teaching, and Leading — Dr. Douglas Reeves

If you liked the tips in this book, Reeves takes them further. Learn how to lead with courage, set teachers up for success, and build a school culture where staff feel supported—not micromanaged. Practical, research-backed, and full of strategies to make your school fearless (and a little less chaotic).

She Leads: The Women's Guide to a Career in Educational Leadership — Dr. Majalise Tolan and Dr. Rachael George

Practical, inspiring guidance for women stepping into leadership roles in education. Full of stories, strategies, and encouragement to lead with confidence, influence, and authenticity.

Meetings & Productivity

The Surprising Science of Meetings — Dr. Steven G. Rogelberg

The Surprising Science of Meetings – Smart, research-based tips to help administrators run meetings that actually matter and don't make everyone want to cry. (Sidenote: as you can tell, I don't love meetings for the sake of meetings.)

A World Without Email: Reimagining Work in an Age of Communication Overload — Cal Newport

A sharp look at how constant emails and messages quietly wreck focus—and sanity—while guiding administrators on reclaiming attention, cutting the noise, and creating better systems that lead to happier, more productive workplaces.

Connection & Well-Being

Together: The Healing Power of Human Connection in a Sometimes Lonely World — Dr. Vivek Murthy

Shows administrators why meaningful connections with staff, students, and colleagues are essential, exploring how loneliness affects our lives and workplaces—and why connection isn't just a "nice to have," it's key to thriving schools and a healthier, happier work life.

My Education Journey

WHY I Wrote This Guide

I was a normal kid—a good student—and had my parents snowed (aka fooled). I was a bit naughty and had too much fun in my high school days. Gina Catherine, and I had a ball and are still friends, going on 47 years. Don't ask me what trouble I got into, but I know it made me a better teacher and administrator. I was (and still am) not perfect—no one is.

Did I always dream of teaching? Ummmm no. I wanted to be a psychologist or a counselor. I accidentally went into education. I was a psych major at U of O (go Ducks, except I now have to say go DAWGS since my youngest is a junior and plays softball at UDub). When I was in high school, a random, amazing returned Peace Corps volunteer (RPCV) gave a presentation on his Peace Corps experience in one of my classes, and I was mesmerized. It was all excitement and adventure. Hell yes, I was doing it. So that's what I did. I applied my junior year at U of O and, luckily, accidentally took too much math (I know, I know), and that sealed the deal. I taught math in French in West Africa. Okay, okay, let's get onto my thankfulness. My main focus is on my colleagues.

I'm thankful for the amazing collaboration, love, and encouragement of my colleagues over the years. Thank you to Thierno Souleymane Baldé. Thierno and I taught and wrote a book together when I was in the Peace Corps in Dabola, Guinea, West Africa. We met there, and he was (and is) one of my best friends. We talked about the crazy customs in each of our countries, laughed, and developed a lifelong friendship. He shared his love for teaching, his life, and his family with me. I ate at his house almost every night, and he never asked for anything. I can still hear his laughter and see his wonderful face. *Tu me manques, mon ami. Je t'aime trop.* He helped me write my mandatory weekly lessons in French which saved me. So dumb! I had to turn them into admin every week.

Thank you, Helen Stapleton, *d'abord.* You and I were the first PCVs in Dabola, and we had some adventures. We played Gin Rummy to 10,000 (I forget who won, probably Helen), traveled to visit other PCVs. I was also mugged, robbed, or burglarized 17 times (stories for another day). My introduction to teaching was cuh-razy, but I fell in love with it anyway. One of the Guinean teachers was skipping work (what?), and parts of the school burned down, so I had to teach in the basketball gym and the movie theater for the first few months of school. Because the other teacher was enjoying coffee, baguettes, and cards with his buddies, I taught 120 seventh graders for a month before the admin found out he was skipping his classes. Oh yes, I taught in French that I had learned in just ten weeks. Overall, it was a life-changing and wonderful experience, and when I returned to the U.S., I became a teacher.

I taught at a few places: an alternative high school in Oregon (most kids were expelled, last-chance education), Hawaii (yes, it was paradise, and I raced outrigger canoes), and eventually back in Oregon. In Hawaii, I met my dear friend Jon Chung. He is like my big brother, and we are still close. He is one of my best friends. He got me interested in the teacher's union, and I was a building rep at the last school I taught in, which helped me immensely as an administrator later.

My father got sick, and I moved back to Oregon. Back in Oregon, I taught middle school at my last teaching job in Beaverton. I'm thankful for my mentors, Teresa Brandon and Glen Rutherford. Both were administrators and were wonderful. Teresa was the second administrator who looked like me. I'm Japanese American, and exactly two of my bosses looked like me in over thirty-three years in education. WTF. Sorry, I digress. That was profoundly powerful for me and encouraged me to believe I could do anything I put my mind to, as long as I worked hard. Glen inspired me—I would have done anything for him. Truly a great leader.

I went to admin school and even though it was lots and lots and lots of theory, my university supervisor was a gem. Gayle Thieman and I still stay in contact, and she is supportive as all get out! I met one of my dearest friends, "Kelley Kelley Kelley" Parosa, in that Monday evening admin cohort. She's the absolute best, truly! Wow, that was hell—teaching all day and then rushing down the highway to my 4:00–9:00 p.m. cohort! At least we got a small break for dinner from a local restaurant. Food always rules.

Sidenote story: I had that Monday cohort every week for months. Class started at 4:00 p.m. and school didn't get out until 3:40 p.m. I had to leave 10 minutes early to make it on time (and even that was a stretch). My nextdoor classroom neighbor was Kristin Hayward. She was (still is!) an incredible English teacher on our team. There was what we called a secret door between our classrooms. She would watch my kids and release them at 3:40 when I had to get to class and leave early on those days. I don't think she knows how much it meant to me that she did that. She always had my back.

As I stated earlier, I was a wee bit naughty in high school, and it's always been funny to me that I spent the majority of my career in administration. I'm also so thankful for Meredith Vandenberg, Gennie Harris, and, as stated earlier, Kristin Hayward. They were my last teacher teammies, and I loved them so very much. We covered for each other, laughed a ton, and had a blast. Getting Taco Bell to-go orders for kids, group chats with chuckle-head students during prep, our interdisciplinary theme park project, and so on. It was the best way to end my teaching career. Once, I won K-103 Teacher of the Week, and the sweetest, most unassuming student nominated me for that award. Her name is Megan, such a hardworking, kind kid. Wow. The things she said about me were things I didn't see in myself, and it still humbles me to this day. Words are powerful. I learned that her view of me wasn't the one I held of myself, but it was real and true for her. We are sometimes unaware of the impact we have on students. That sounds strange, but teachers hold an enormous amount of responsibility in the lives of students and families.

Side note: I thought Meredith was pranking me when the radio station called. I may have cussed a tiny bit and told her to shut the f***k up. Ha.

Meredith used to give me crap about "going to the dark side." I asked her, "Wouldn't you want someone like me on the dark side?" She paused, thought about it, and said yes. She gave me two figurines I had to promise to display in my office: Yoda and Darth

Mar. I also had to promise I would never forget to "see the light." Meredith, I had those figurines in both offices at the two high schools where I served as an administrator. They were both on a shelf in all my offices. When I left administration in 2023, I passed Yoda and Darth Mar on to an aspiring administrator, JD Bellum, to display when he becomes an admin, because I know he will be a great one. I miss working and laughing with him. He is incredibly smart and any school that hires him will be getting gold. I hope he always believes in himself and doesn't give up on pursuing an administrator role. I would have loved to work alongside him as a fellow admin.

Eventually, I took an administrator job with a 45- to 90-minute commute, depending on traffic. I loved the staff, the students, and the fast pace. The commute nearly killed me, and that may have been because my kids were one and four years old when I left after two and a half years. I was hired midyear and processed roughly 1,800 referrals a year in a school of 1,900 students. I'm deeply thankful for Sam Ragaisis. She was a lifesaver as a new administrator, and we stayed close for many years despite only working together for one short year. She is an incredible person and administrator, and one I aspired to be like, even though I never quite reached her level.

Then I landed at my dream school. Truly, the best school anywhere. I loved it there. The students, the families, the staff. Everything. Eventually, we moved our family to that town, and both of my daughters attended the school. A dream. Our first admin team, Pat Johnson, Dennis Burke, and John Ogden, had a lot of work ahead of us, and we were a strong team. I learned from each of them and am grateful for the values they helped solidify. They were all former coaches, and I'll admit my eyes glazed over when sports talk started, but they gave me excellent advice about my kids. We still laugh about how little I understand sports.

Over the years, we made meaningful progress building culture and collaboration. Working in a place you love, with people you trust and who trust you, is the ultimate goal in education. In 2017, I was named Assistant Principal of the Year in Oregon. It shocked me. The Coalition of School Administrators and my principal, Greg Dinse, surprised me with the announcement at an early morning staff meeting. Like most educators, I struggle with imposter syndrome, and I didn't feel worthy. Then my colleagues gave me a standing ovation.

Thank you to my former principal, Greg Dinse—former FBI agent, retired lieutenant colonel in the Marine Corps, social studies teacher, friend, and bagpiper. Not many people bring that résumé to a school. I will never forget him bagpiping the freshmen into school on their first day and again at graduation—a special full-circle moment for all of us.

I'm also deeply thankful for John Ogden. We worked together at two different schools, oddly both with long commutes. He is the epitome of positivity and joy. We used to call him Odie (for us old-timers), he was the cartoon character Garfield's happy buddy. You don't know Garfield and Odie, oh the power of the internet, go look them up! John and I were like brother and sister and it was so much fun working with him. When I had my youngest daughter, he brought us a pizza to the hospital. I highly recommend–10/10!

He is one of my closest friends and one of the kindest humans I know. Truly one in a million.

Jamie Netter deserves multiple paragraphs. She was my partner in crime, an extraordinary educator, and someone who gives her whole heart to people. I'll curse anyone who isn't on Jamie's side. She is phenomenal, sassy as hell in the best way, and I miss belly laughing with her more than I can say. I'll ride at dawn any day for her—she's just the hardest working, most loving person ever.

I miss the staff and amazing community we had. So many brilliant, kind, funny, sometimes chaotic, and deeply committed people. I love them, most of them. Kathy Rogers, Ethyl, made me laugh daily. Her pies were to die for… Erika Shearer had endless energy, truly an Energizer Bunny. Sue Winner, pee-my-pants funny, and I'm thrilled she got to retire at the end of last school year. We were both core members of the Sunshine Committee.

I'm also thankful for the final admin team I worked with: Cari Sloan, Ben Winegar, and Megan Jackson.

Working with Ben was a full-circle moment. I supervised him as a science teacher, and he later became an administrator. He is smart, energetic, kind, and feels like a kid brother.

Megan and I only worked together for one year, but what a year it was. She's pure sunshine—any school is better because she's in it. Her heart is 100% for students and staff, and wherever she lands as a principal will be one lucky community. I just wish we'd had more time together. She's truly a gem.

Cari was the last building principal I worked for. I loved making her laugh, she did not love hugs so I tried to sneak in a hug every so often. She's also an English teacher and helped me with my writing (insert hug emoji). I have no doubt that when she becomes a university professor, she'll shape some incredible teachers.

I "graduated" from administration when my youngest daughter graduated in 2023. I was tired of working twelve to sixteen hour days and most weekends. Gosh, I loved my school, a great community, kick ass kids and amazing colleagues.

I then became a new teacher mentor for teachers working with students who have complex disabilities in a countywide program. My new position was a certified/licensed position, I was not an administrator. I loved my colleagues during the year and a half I was there. Those educators, teachers, related service providers, and paraprofessionals have the hardest jobs I've ever seen. The staff was outstanding. My experience with the program administration was not great.

Turnover exceeded forty percent if you included contracted staff. People felt micromanaged, unsupported, and unheard. I got in more trouble during that short time as a TOSA than in my previous 32 years combined, often for absurd reasons. I was reprimanded for planning laser tag with colleagues for team building because it wasn't "in my job description." When asked why I would do that, I said, "Because it's fun and builds relationships." They said they'd also talk to the other staff involved. They never did. And honestly, I didn't care because it was a dumb reason for us to get in trouble.

I was told I could no longer eat lunch with my mentees. Other staff were discouraged from coming to me for help. I wasn't allowed to coach teachers on how to work with challenging educational assistants and had to refer them to administrators. Everything was micromanaged. It was suffocating.

Despite that, I met incredible people and still stay in touch with many of them. Jesse Eggleston-Black and Amy Fredrickson are phenomenal teachers and humans. Amy is also my workout buddy, she is very motivating! Jesse is just Jesse—someone I will keep in touch with forever. Richard Lee is an aspiring administrator who will absolutely rock wherever he lands. He is hardworking, generous, and an asset to any program.

I always believed my primary role as an administrator was to support teachers so they could teach. I assumed that was universal: support staff, manage students and parents, trust people, communicate clearly, be transparent, listen, be present, avoid bias, assume best intent, and put students first. Wow, talk about being naive!

That wasn't the experience staff (or I) had in that program. People feared retribution for honest feedback. Multiple staff shared that administrators could—and did—identify who wrote survey comments, and people were punished for it. I saw it firsthand. Surveys were collected, but feedback was never shared and no action was taken. Meanwhile, other departments shared results and made changes. Their staff felt valued by their administrators. Ours felt ignored—or worse, punished. The good news? Leadership changed the next school year.

That experience was painful, eye-opening, and ultimately clarifying. It's one of the reasons I wrote this guide (yes, fueled by rage fire): to help new administrators serve staff, students, families, and organizations with integrity, humanity, humility, and care. No one person is above another. Relationships are KEY.

Above all, serve with:

- An open mind
- A kind heart
- A genuine desire to help others
- The courage to say no
- The humility to recognize your own bias

Not too difficult, right?

I'm rooting for you. You've got this!

And just to be clear ... I don't believe administration is the "dark side." Not if you do it the right way.

"To be Jedi is to face the truth, and choose.
Give off light or darkness, ... Be a candle or the night."
~Yoda

Appendix | Odds and Ends

Here are a bunch of random stuff … hopefully helpful to you!

Do a web search for:

Student Check-in Supplies

- Folio Notebook - should be around $16
- Portable File Box - should be around $13 - $16

Observation Tools

- iWalk Observation
- Google Docs/Sheets Templates (make a copy to edit)

Templates mentioned in this guide:

- Hump Day Bump Form Template: https://bit.ly/4sZ4UhM
- Student Check-In Sheet: https://bit.ly/4sqFgCD
- Phone Log Template: https://bit.ly/4cZrS3B
- Goals/Observations Template: https://bit.ly/4ssxfgx
- Abbreviations: https://bit.ly/3PlUrhW

A Few More Thank Yous

My copy editor was kind, funny, and brutal—in the best way. I'm grateful to Jen Zelinger Marshall for being wonderfully "heavy-handed" with my manuscript.

Thank you to my proofreaders, Theresa Kahl and Lisa Just, for catching things I missed. Theresa made me laugh when she corrected my *for fucks sake* to *for fuck's sake*—especially funny coming from someone who does not cuss at all. Lisa, you're such a pretty princess—love you! Thank you for your questions and constant encouragement.

Mia Carroll, my beloved daughter, her Canva magic made this book look good! She can do just about anything!

Huge thanks to my early endorsers—Douglas Reeves, Marnie Stockman, Majalise Tolan, Jovan Jones, and Alexis Frixione. They took the time to read, give honest feedback, and hype this book up—I appreciate you all!

Thank you to my audio book designer Rebecca Finkel for my "final final fixes" and for her patience and understanding from this new author!

And thank you to my book designer, Nick Zelinger—just as wonderful as his daughter, Jen—for his kindness, help, and patience with my many questions.

Finally, to the teachers and staff who show up every day for kids—this book is for you.

You and your students deserve great leadership.

www.ingramcontent.com/pod-product-compliance
Lightning Source LLC
LaVergne TN
LVHW021159160826
845679LV00024B/2168

9798995578307